Dates for Mates

Romancing the One You Love

Faith Marriage is an imprint of Cook Communications Ministries, Colorado Springs, Colorado 80918
Cook Communications, Paris, Ontario
Kingsway Communications, Eastbourne, England

Other LifeMates products available from Cook Communications Ministries:

LifeMates by Dave and Jan Congo
They Call Me Mr. Romance by Mike Keyes

Coming SUMMER 2002:
   Inspiring Dates for Lasting Mates
   Walking with God Together

Dates for Mates
© 2001 by Lisa Keyes and Debbie Black.
All rights reserved.

1 2 3 4 5 6 7 8 9 10 Printing/Year 05 04 03 02 01

Senior Editor: Janet Lee
Design: Image Studios
Cartoon Illustrations: Mary Chambers

Library of Congress Cataloging-in-Publication Data
Applied for
ISBN 0781436907

LIFEMATES
SERIES

Dates for Mates

Romancing the One You Love

Lisa Keyes and Debbie Black

FAITH Marriage

Love. Honor. Cherish
faithmarriage.com

Dedications

To the many couples who have shared
their stories in this book. Thank you
for your honesty, your efforts, and your
commitment. We wish you many
happy years of dating together.

—Lisa and Debbie

To Thom, my husband of 25 years,
who still makes me laugh!

—Debbie

To my husband Michael who, after 16
years of marriage, is still my best friend.
Thanks for making my life
a daily adventure. I love you.

—Lisa

"If you live to be a hundred,
I want to be a hundred minus one day,
So that I never have to
live without you."

Christopher Robin to Winnie the Pooh

Table of Contents

Introduction 11

The "Dating" Thing 17

Burning Romance 21

That "Other" Hawaii 25

Romance at the Diner 31

Can We Fall in Love Again? 37

Celebrating the Big One 41

The Turning Point 47

A Picnic with the Doctor 53

Beatin' the Travelin' Man Blues 57

Bubble Memories 63

Cupid Has Arrived 67

Our Night In 71

Antique Love 77

Protecting Our Time 81

Do I Know You? 85

Strength for the Storm 91

Romance after Twins 95

December in Hartford 101

That Newlywed Feeling 107

Something out of Nothing 111

Seeing with New Eyes 117

Somewhere in Time 123

Introduction

How often we reminisce.

Those romantic days before things got too familiar. The days when we called each other constantly. Things were busy, but our desire to connect was so strong it didn't matter. Connecting was most important, whatever way we did it. And the weekends. Oh, the weekends. A time when the rest of the world ended, and we spent endless time talking, kissing, and connecting. Dates were set, perfume donned, and our best clothes were pulled out of the closet. We did anything to impress and woo.

When we went out no one else existed in the whole restaurant. The movie playing was just for the two of us. We held hands constantly and never ran out of things to talk about. Meeting for a two-hour breakfast and combing through the

Sunday paper together was a must. There was never too much time devoted to romance.

Where did those days go? How did they slip away? When did the job, the kids, the commitments, the sports, even all the charity and church work we do become so all important that we put the connection time with our partner aside so easily? No doubt it happened so subtly we didn't even notice. Now we look at the person passing us in the hallway, and we realize we don't even know what makes him or her happy anymore. It has been so long since the two of us met longer than the time it took to match up calendars that we don't even know how to act with each other in a romantic sense. How quickly it all happens.

We've been there. We fell into this trap so quickly we didn't even see it coming. Jobs consumed us. Of course, we could understand that. Running our own company took extra time. And we couldn't neglect that. Then came the kids. Everyone accepts the importance of being there for the kids. Thousands of books today emphasize the need for us to be there for our kids, available to support and encourage the growth of these perfect little humans. And of course we needed to be involved in school. We didn't want to miss out on that. Then came all that charity and church work. A chance to give back for all that we have received. All these important things. How we wanted to be a part of them. But to what consequence? Are we making a sacrifice we can no longer afford?

Husbands and wives today not only find that their time to connect is minimal, but even thinking of a way to connect can be overwhelming. And we wonder why our marriages are dissolving at a record rate. Where did we go wrong?

Alas, romance does not have to die. Hollywood's idea of the perfect date may not exist anymore, but married couples are still dating. Yes, the traditional date may not be so traditional any more but couples who do date are making it a priority to connect in any way they can. We have collected in this book real stories that reflect some of the different ways couples are molding their dating life to fit the different circumstances and stages of their lives.

These stories may not make it into the record books, but they are about real people who are making a real effort to make the connection that today's marriages so desperately need. They are stories that will inspire you, encourage you, make you laugh, make you cry, and most of all make you think. As you read these stories, move beyond the actual people and their lives. Let these stories motivate you to take that first step to bring dating back into your marriage.

Don't be discouraged because you don't have the money, the time, or the creativity to think up fifty-two of the most memorable and exciting dates. You can still connect in your marriage. The people in these stories are no different than you. They have busy lives, full of commitments. But they have made a choice. A choice to make their marriage a priority. A choice to develop a friendship and a partnership that will remain strong through difficulties, through challenges—throughout a lifetime.

We hope these stories will encourage you to take a step toward developing a new connection with your LifeMate.

Never underestimate the power of a good date.
A good date has been known to
salvage crippled relationships,
reunite lost partners,
bring focus to confused spouses,
rekindle disappointed lovers,
encourage hopeless mates,
and provide a fresh start to couples longing
to recapture the passion

Never, never, underestimate the power
of a good date.

SO... ARE YOU BUSY NEXT THURSDAY NIGHT?

The "Dating" Thing
One

Midway through our marriage, I realized I wasn't being a very good husband. Nicole, bearing much of the parental burden of raising two children in the early elementary school years, needed a husband who would participate in two-way communication, not just mutter one-sided monologues. Then I heard a speaker challenge husbands to date their wives regularly. He stated, "If your wife isn't scheduled on your weekly calendar, don't tell me she's important to you." His statement was pretty convicting so I resolved to date my wife after years of sliding by.

I surprised Nicole one evening by bringing up the topic, and she responded enthusiastically to my idea that we go out to a restaurant regularly. But then we looked at our budget. The cost of eating out at a decent restaurant and paying for a sitter would definitely put a big dent in our finances, which already left little room for "frills."

The more I thought about this dating thing, the more I knew we should do this. Nicole and I needed to connect. We needed time just to sit and talk about our lives, and our future. We needed time to let each other know we still cared for and appreciated each other. I just didn't want to go into credit card debt to make it happen.

Then we came up with a solution: the lunch date. Since we lived less than fifteen minutes from my work, Nicole could come to my downtown office, and from there, we could walk a city block or two to a nice restaurant. We even purchased an Entertainment Book, which is an encyclopedia of "two-for-one" discount coupons to local eateries. And the added bonus—no sitter fees because the kids were in school!

I began to look forward to those lunch dates. Seeing Nicole walk into my place of work brightened my day. She always dressed up to make the event special, so I knew she also looked forward to our rendezvous. I liked walking several city blocks with her and enjoying our intimate conversations amidst the corporate environment. And the price? Well, let's just say that we could afford to make our lunch dates a regular occurrence. Our relationship improved. Our communication became better. Our knowledge of where to find the best Chinese food exploded. And it all happened because we decided that dating needed to hold a significant place in our relationship.

Mike and Nicole Yorkey
Married May 18, 1979

When was the last time you truly connected as a couple? Isn't it time you made a commitment to date again?

This couple made that commitment, and it changed their marriage. Plus they did it in a way that fit into their lifestyle and their budget.

Dating is an essential part of a marriage.

It requires our utmost attention.

It makes sense.

If you aren't dating your mate, it's time to start. Sit down together and make a plan.

You will see a miracle happen in your marriage that you couldn't imagine.

Before long, you won't be able to imagine life without that time of connection and intimacy.

Before long you'll find you've fallen in love all over again.

Two
Burning Romance

It was a time of stress in our marriage. We hadn't been married long, but our life was already in turmoil. In addition to being a new bride, I also had become an instant mom to my husband's one-year-old son. I was busy finishing my undergraduate classes as my husband was in the midst of law school. On top of that, both of us were working. We had a lot on our plates and learning how to be married was just too difficult at times. We already had experienced far too many ups' and downs' in our short marriage.

Fortunately, my husband decided to step up to the plate and make an effort to get our marriage connected. He came to me one day, asking me to drive with him to the airport to pick up a friend. It seemed strange, but I went. Everything seemed even stranger to me when he pulled into the long-term parking area just to pick up his friend. Well, things became a little clearer as John opened the trunk and revealed a suitcase, all packed and ready to go. He hugged me and told me he was whisking me away to Cabo San Lucas, Mexico for three wonderful, romantic days. Wow! I couldn't believe he had gone to all this trouble for me.

We arrived in Cabo and couldn't wait to get our little white bodies out into the hot, baking sun! As we lay there basking for hours, enjoying the scenery and time together, we had no idea of the sunburn we were developing. By the time we returned to our room, we looked like boiled lobsters! Not only were we burned, but we both suffered from heatstroke and felt terrible.

Somehow, this romantic interlude had taken an unexpected turn. We couldn't do much except hang out in our room and talk. . . and talk. . . and talk. Needless to say, we made up for all the hours our busy schedules had stolen from us. We reconnected.

That trip didn't turn out to be the romantic holiday my husband had planned, but who could have imagined the growth and connection that came out of that time together? To many this trip may seem to have been a disaster. Yet it changed our marriage forever and from that time on we pledged to make a consistent time to communicate in our marriage.

We may not always have the chance to go away to a beautiful beach and bake in the sun, but we can make the time to develop sweet memories wherever we are and whatever circumstances we may face.

John and Kimberley Mendoza
Married May 18, 1986

What is your idea of connection time?
Do you feel you must have everything
perfectly in order to connect?
Sometimes even the best-laid plans can fall apart.
But we still can make the choice to connect.

Try to make each moment together an opportunity to
learn what is happening in your spouse's life. Don't let
your marriage get lost in a hectic world. Make the time
to remember whom it is you married, whether it be on a
romantic beach or at a local seafood joint.

It isn't where you go, but what you do with the
time you have together.

Help for the Husband Planning a Get-Away

If you are planning to surprise your wife with a trip out of town, you may want to enlist the help of one of your wife's good friends. She can help you decide what to take, and she could review the activities for the children and help make any necessary adjustments or arrangements.

Use this checklist for reference:

- Don't forget to pack your wife's makeup and any special toiletries. This will make her feel more comfortable on the trip.
- Make a list for the person watching your kids of all emergency phone numbers and a second contact person who knows the ins and outs of your home.
- Make arrangements for any carpooling needs.
- Make a schedule of bedtimes, mealtimes, routines, etc. for the person watching the kids.

- Don't forget to make arrangements for meals. Either   leave money for take-out or shop for necessary groceries.
- Leave a list of your children's important friends' phone numbers and their parents' names.
- Remember your wife's special pillow. She will love you for it.

If you have never left your children like this before, reassure them and remind them that this is a special time for Mom. Your calm explanation will help avoid crying phone calls and a distracted mom who can't enjoy the getaway.

Three
Hawaii in Disguise

It didn't take long for my husband to start making a commitment to connect in our marriage. On our first anniversary he began a special tradition. For weeks he planned a special getaway to a local California beach town, only two hours away by car. He picked the hotel, planned the meals, and even packed my bags—a major feat for any man! He picked me up from work and headed north in the car on the first of our many "mystery getaways."

The most memorable, although not necessarily the most romantic, of our "mystery getaways" took place on our third anniversary. Robin, a native of the dreary country of England had planned an island getaway to Catalina Island. Well, anyone growing up in England might be under the false impression that Catalina was just a smaller version of Hawaii, and my husband was no exception. He had visions of endless palm trees, white sand beaches, and bikini-clad islanders serving drinks poolside. This is definitely *not* the case on Catalina!

At this point in our marriage, I was pregnant with our first child, and, in this stage of my motherhood adventure, I had become the best of friends with the toilet. Therefore, when we arrived at the port of Newport, ready to board the cruiser to the island, I wondered if I would make a widower of my husband on this trip. The ride over was truly an adventure and, from what I hear, quite beautiful. And to think I needed to return on this thing in a few short days!

When we arrived at the island port, the reality that this was not the "other" Hawaii had finally hit my sweet British husband. Vowing to make the best of it, we headed off to our romantic cabana, nestled in a tiny community. As we entered our room, the "best" room in the hotel, we were overwhelmed! The room was, well, a dump. We couldn't believe we were going to spend four whole days in this place!

About the time we decided to settle in, my stomach decided to become unsettled so I chose to rest up for the afternoon. I turned on the TV just as the events of "Baby Jessica in the Well" began to unfold. Needless to say, any thoughts of romance went right out the window as I, in my early stages of motherhood, became immersed in the plight of this poor woman and her child.

Robin gave up and headed out to explore. Hours later he returned to find me in the same place, watching the same tragedy. All was not lost, though, as he began to replay for me stories about the locals he had spent the afternoon with at the local pier. We laughed hysterically as he described the crusty sea captains and the antics of the local bar crowd. Finally, we mustered the energy to vacate our little palace to take our own stroll through the town together. It wasn't long before we made true memories.

This may not have been the most romantic time Robin and I have spent together, but it became one of our most humorous memories. We learned so much about each other on that trip. And connecting at that time in our lives, just before being hit with the commitments of parenting, strengthened us.

Thankfully the downfalls of the trip didn't discourage my husband from planning our future trips. In fact, he has never missed a year. Recently, he surprised me for our ten-year anniversary, and guess what—we made it to the real island of Hawaii.

As our two girls continue to grow, so does our busy schedule. The commitments in our lives can, at times, be overwhelming. Yet our yearly getaway gives us that true connection time we need to keep our marriage in perspective. When times get tough and connection starts to slip, I remind myself of the incredible times we have had on these trips and I anticipate with longing our next "mystery getaway."

Robin and Teri Gable
Married October 15, 1985

What about you?
Do you have a tradition in your marriage?

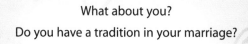

A tradition can take on many forms. It might be returning
each year to a special place that holds a unique memory for
you and your spouse.
Or it might mean going on a picnic the
first day of summer each year.

Maybe he can surprise her with a traditional "last
Thursday of the month" lunch date.
Maybe she could plan a hike every May Day.

Whatever your taste, you can make a tradition.
It doesn't have to be as elaborate as a yearly "mystery get-
away," but it can become your tradition.
Why not start one today?

WHAT I REALLY NEED IS A VACATION SO PERFECT I NEVER HAVE TO DO THIS AGAIN

29

Four
Romance at the Diner

After eighteen years of marriage, Rob and I have been on some fabulous trips and evenings on the town, but most of these were before the birth of our two children. Since parenthood, these types of romantic outings have become few and far between.

Like many parents, we struggle financially to provide our children with a good home and a good education. We also spend an inordinate amount of time carpooling, helping with homework, making costumes, attending kids sporting events and vocal performances, cooking meals, packing lunches, and washing load after load of laundry. Additionally, I work full-time during the day, running my own business, and my husband has spent the last six years working the night shift as an editor for the city paper.

DATES FOR MATES

We discovered we spent most of our "connection" time recapping schedules and confirming future appointments. So many times when Rob was working night shift, I would only see him for a few minutes a day, and these minutes were definitely not "quality time." What little spare time we had left over at the end of a hectic day, week, or month, we spent either at a cultural event (so our brains didn't atrophy), or with our children on a family outing or vacation.

We began to realize that if we were going to have quality connection time, we had to become creative. When we were first married, a very wise person told us that as our lives became more frenzied with children, work, and financial obligations, we would have to work harder to uphold the commitment of marriage. In addition to lots of suggestions on how to connect, he asked us to consider locking ourselves in a closet for thirty minutes once a week in order to get time alone. We laughed at this suggestion, thinking that our lives would never come to that! However, I must admit that this idea doesn't sound far-fetched anymore!

Since the closet idea seemed a little desperate, we decided to come up with our own version—a practical way to connect, despite our mismatched schedules so that our marriage did not slip away from us. We discussed what type of smaller, simpler dates we could go on that would remind us how much we loved each other and why we wanted to stay together. One particular idea came to mind.

Rob started calling me at least once a month to ask me out for lunch. He would drive down to my office, and we went out for a $5.00 lunch at the local diner. Sitting among the truck drivers and construction workers and eating corn beef sandwiches or "Joe's Specials," we reconnected with one another. We talked about our lives, not just the day-to-day grind.

We talked about our future goals and what we wanted from our jobs. We imagined what our lives would be like after our children grew up and moved out, and we even fantasized about future trips to exotic locations.

Those lunch dates became a critical part of maintaining the romance in our marriage during such a hectic time. It is amazing to think that on a shoestring budget, in a non-romantic location, that one-hour together did as much for us as a vacation in Hawaii.

Now Rob is back on day shift, and I find myself missing our lunch dates. We have more time now to go out in the evening, but when we do, we tend to go to the movies or the theater where we really don't talk. I think we need to reinstate our lunch dates. If not, Rob may find himself locked in the closet with me!

Rob and Cathy Davila
Married October 30, 1982

Do both you and your spouse work?
Maybe even on opposite schedules?
This can add an extra stumbling block in making that
connection time. Connecting will take more creativity
and, at times, a lot more effort.

But that time and effort is worth it. Lunch at the local
diner or coffee together between shifts may be the one
thing that holds your marriage together.

Don't put off making time to connect by thinking
that this phase of your life won't last forever. Before you
know it, weeks turn into months, and months turn into
years and that time to connect has slipped away.
Take back the time and make the effort. It will be
worth it in the long run.

Top 10

Things to Say on a Date

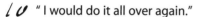

10 " I would do it all over again."

9 "You look younger every day."

8 "I think this is the best our marriage has ever been."

7 "I love what you are doing with your hair."

6 "I want to know what you think."

5 "Have I ever told you why I appreciate you?"

4 "Will you forgive me for being so stupid?"

3 "You are sexier now than when we got married."

2 "We need to do this again."

1 "I love you. I really do."

Five
Can We Fall in Love again?

Only ten weeks after my wife, Krickett, and I were married, we were involved in a tragic car accident in which Krickett suffered a severe skull fracture. One of the results of her injuries was that Krickett no longer had any short-term memory. She had no recollection of the previous eighteen months of her life, the part of her life that included our marriage and me.

Krickett became involved in many weeks of therapy, or "school," as she called it, in Phoenix, Arizona. I, however, still lived in Las Vegas, New Mexico, where I worked as the coach of the New Mexico Highlands University baseball team.

During this difficult time, the community of Las Vegas raised enough money for me to make ten round trips to visit Krickett. That meant I could see my wife every week and be involved in her therapy. Sadly, Krickett grew to resent my pushing her in therapy, and we began to grow farther and farther apart. I wondered if I would ever get my life with my wife back again.

One week I was unable to make the trip to visit Krickett because the baseball team I coached was heading into play-offs. So, instead, I called her each night to see how her day had been and what happened in "school" that day. It was my way of trying to make some kind of a connection—a makeshift date with my wife.

Unfortunately, there was no emotion in her heart for me, and I was becoming very discouraged. It was clear that even talking to me at all was hard for Krickett. One night I stayed late at the ball field, getting things ready for the team to leave the next day on a road trip. When I arrived home, I didn't want to chance calling and waking Krickett, so I decided to wait until the next evening. Soon the phone rang and I picked it up to hear my mother-in-law on the other end, telling me someone wanted to speak to me. Next, Krickett came on the line: "I just wanted to say hi. I've got to go now. Bye."

One little phone call changed everything. We had finally made a connection. I now had the first glimpse of hope that Krickett and I were going to make it.

Many wouldn't classify those little phone calls as dates, but for me they were the one way in Krickett and I could connect during such a difficult time. When Krickett called me that evening, it became the best date I had ever had. It was the date that gave our marriage hope.

I re-dated my wife over the next several months and, thankfully, she fell in love with me again. We had another wedding ceremony in which we began a new marriage. Soon after we had a baby boy. Today we both still hold dear each opportunity, no matter how simple, to connect and enhance our commitment to each other. Each moment, including those on the phone, are unique chances to remind each other of our lifetime love for one another.

Kim and Krickett Carpenter
Married September 18, 1993 and May 25,1996

Many of us face times in our marriages when we aren't sure we want to go on. Maybe the emotion is so far gone that even speaking to each other is difficult.
Don't give up.

Luckily, in this story, Kim still held on to a little hope and persevered. Look for the littlest glimmer that even the smallest of connections might reveal. It doesn't always have to be a big revelation that pulls us back together again. It might be just a phone call or a look.
Don't miss it.

It will take time and commitment. Recommit yourself to dating your mate in any way that works for you, taking it a step at a time.
Rekindle that love that once drew you together.

Remember the miracle of Kim and Krickett's marriage.
Your marriage is valuable—don't give up on it Give it a try!

SIX
celebrating the Big One

As our fifteenth anniversary approached, we began to feel pressure. You know, that pressure that comes from everyone asking, "So what special plans have you made to celebrate the 'big' anniversary?" It seemed everyone wanted to know where we were going or what we would be doing to mark this special occasion.

But that summer, as in many summers past, the special trip, evening, or whatever, was far beyond our reach. My husband was in the midst of starting a new company; therefore time, finances, and creative juices were either very tight or non-existent. Add to this the fact that our anniversary was sandwiched between three other family birthdays, all within a three-week period, and you'll understand why we were feeling overwhelmed.

DATES FOR MATES

Although we tried to put it off, our "big" anniversary was soon upon us, and we had no plans. Every restaurant my husband tried for a reservation at the last minute was booked. And the thought of just going to a movie was too depressing. So at 6:00 p.m. I headed off to get a sitter, knowing we had no idea what we were going to do. As I drove, I began to pray—that was all I had left to do. I asked God to give us a night to remember.

When I got home, an idea came to me. Our first date had been to a local beach town where we walked and talked for hours. Although it was a busy time of year there, I suggested we drive in that direction with hopes of finding somewhere to eat. It was then that the miracles started to unfold. As we drove up the coast, we saw in the sky above us a skywriter, making heart shapes in the air! We looked at those hearts the whole way into town and enjoyed that little gift of romance from heaven.

Once in town, we knew parking would be a problem because the big art festival was in full swing. But just as we drove up a little street, a spot was waiting for us, with no meter! We walked to a well-known restaurant that was always crowded, hoping beyond hope that we could get in. The maître d' not only had a table, but he even offered to hold it for us so we could walk around town first. When we returned forty-five minutes later, a special table by the window was waiting for us.

The food and the atmosphere were wonderful. Could anything spoil our special evening? Well, maybe just one little thing. As we were enjoying the scrumptious soufflé for dessert, we discovered a small piece of wire mesh on the side. The maître d' apologized profusely. Then he presented us with a certificate for a free dinner in the future! This was working out far too well.

The most gorgeous moon we'd ever seen highlighted our drive home and, yes, it was in front of us the whole way. Could we have planned a more romantic evening? Maybe. But we experienced great joy because we went into that evening with open hearts, deciding not to live by everyone else's expectations. We simply went on our date with the desire to connect and reflect.

God answered my prayer with an incredibly memorable date, and in addition, He reconfirmed His hand in our marriage.

Mike and Lisa Keyes
Married August 17, 1985

Do you fall prey to everyone else's idea of
what a proper date should be?
So often we are overwhelmed with the pressure of planning
what the world says is
the "perfect" date?
But how often do you turn your dates over to the
One who has the biggest interest in your marriage?
Only God can provide that unique date that is
custom-made for your marriage.
Why don't you ask Him for His involvement
in your dates?

God may come up with something better than
even the best movie writer could create.

Let Go and Be Surprised

The greatest enemy to a wonderful date is
unrealistic expectations.
Don't put so much pressure on yourselves.
Once the plans have been made, let go.
Enjoy the moment and the experience as it comes to you.

Maybe you're on the way to a hotel, and you get a flat.
You have to change the tire in the rain.
What, the hotel lost your reservation?

Whatever.

It's still a Date.

Your date.
Somehow, through it all, remember that this is your
opportunity to spend time together, to communicate,
to laugh, maybe even to cry.

It's your time.

Don't let your expectations and your desire for perfection
ruin the moment gifted to you.
Be surprised.
Maybe you will come up with a good story for
the grandkids.

Seven
The Turning Point

We had been separated almost one month when Mark called and asked me if I wanted to go to church with him. I was a little surprised and not sure what he was thinking, but I agreed to go. He picked me up and suggested we might go to brunch (my favorite Sunday thing to do) after church. Although hesitant, I decided to stay relaxed and just let the day unfold.

The service seemed to be directed right toward us that morning, and I could tell as we walked out that Mark was as affected by the sermon as I was. We walked out without saying anything, passing right by the marriage ministry table. Suddenly Mark stopped. Then he looked right at me and said, "Do you want to go to the LifeMates event tonight?" We had talked about going some time, but we had never actually attended. Somewhat in shock, I agreed to go to the event with Mark. We went back to the marriage ministry table and bought tickets.

After church we went to a nice restaurant at the beach and had a delicious brunch while looking out at the harbor. We started talking about this and that and even laughed a little. I remember thinking that even though we weren't going to stay together, this was a good way to end our marriage on friendly terms. The ice broken, we left brunch and Mark led me down toward the water.

We sat down on a bench and looked at the boats. It was a beautiful day with a softly blowing wind. Mark put his arm along the back of the bench and started talking to me right from his heart. We sat there for hours. I had no expectations, but I appreciated his honesty and sincerity as he spoke of what had happened to him and inside him during the weeks we were separated. I listened to him intently until it was time to head back to church for LifeMates.

I had no idea what to expect when we walked up to the worship center, but I certainly didn't expect to see everyone dressed up and the worship center transformed into what looked like a beautiful wedding reception! We went in and immediately bumped into the main speaker, my former marriage counselor. She knew what was ahead that night and looked a little nervous for us. We soon found out why.

Mark and I enjoyed the skits, talks, and everything else, but the shock came when the pastor began to talk about the vow renewal in which we would all participate. I wanted to stand up and run out of the building. I was sure we'd be the only couple who did not participate in this very tender moment. But when the pastor called for the couples wanting to renew their vows to stand up, much to my surprise, Mark stood up, turned to me, and held out his hand to help me stand up next to him. (Believe me, I needed help standing up.) I looked into his eyes, and I could tell he knew exactly what he was about to do.

When Mark began to repeat the vows along with all the other men in the room, he struggled to speak audibly. His tears spoke volumes. I can't really remember how I did when it was time for me to repeat my vows to Mark. I do, however, remember sensing with absolute certainty that God was with us every moment of that day, guiding us through to the point where we were reunited, under Him, stronger than ever.

Teri and Mark Goodwin
Married June 12, 1998

Is your marriage in a dark time right now?
You are not alone
When was the last time you went out on a limb and made the
first move to reconnect
in your marriage?
Are you open to what could happen
on just one date?
This couple didn't know
what lay ahead for them
on this date, but they were open.
This one date changed their marriage forever.

Don't give up!
Miracles happen everyday.
Maybe one is just around the corner for you.

Whether it is separation, illness,
a death in the family, or something
else is casting a shadow on
your marriage, take a chance
and make the effort to reconnect.
One date could be the light that shines a new
perspective on the darkness in your marriage.

I'M SORRY, RUSSELL. IT JUST DOESN'T SEEM RIGHT TO KISS ON OUR FIRST DATE—EVEN IF WE _ARE_ MARRIED.

Eight

A Picnic with the Doctor

Years ago my husband was working on his doctorate and also working full-time as a counselor. This obviously left us with very little time together. Many weeks we would hardly see each other for days. I remember a period of several particularly intense weeks when I was missing my husband. There was a battle raging inside of me. Part of me was thinking, Why does this have to be so tough? Does he really care? Another side of me was urging me to do something to bridge the gap. That side won out.

I came up with a great idea. I phoned the secretary at the counseling office where my husband worked, and I scheduled myself under a different name as a new client. The secretary didn't recognize my voice so she was not able to give me away to my husband. On the appointed day, I arrived holding a picnic basket with some of my husband's favorites packed neatly inside. I'm sure you can imagine the surprise on the secretary's face when a woman walked into a therapy appointment with a picnic basket.

But more exciting was the look on my husband's face when he came out to get his "new client." He was shocked. Together we went into his office and enjoyed an uninterrupted hour together. We spread out a blanket and enjoyed a wonderful lunch. We shared funny stories and caught up on things we had put aside for too long. Was it enough? NO. We both wanted more. But it was a start, and it gave us just enough encouragement to keep going in difficult times.

Dave and Jan Congo
Married August 7, 1971

Is your marriage passing you by?
Are you spending your time in anger over what isn't happening or has never been?
Instead of harboring anger over a mate consumed by work
and neglectful of you, why not take the bull by the horns
and make plans yourself for the two of you?

It's amazing what a change in direction can accomplish.
Maybe by making the first move, you can ignite a spark that
will set your marriage on fire!
Stubbornness will never make a marriage.
Let go of your pride and take the challenge.

Pack that picnic basket and make that appointment now.
It could be the best appointment you ever made.

Nine
Beatin' The Travelin' Man Blues

I am blessed to be married to a sensational man. He is fun to be around, encouraging, confident, an involved father, and a loving husband. The problem? He travels. A LOT! It is not unusual for him to be traveling three weeks a month. This poses quite a dilemma for us. And when he is in town, he wants to stay home, but I am itching to get out!

However, I have found that grumbling does little good because in his line of work, traveling is a necessity. Complaining about the travel just creates an atmosphere of negativity. Instead, my solution is quite simple: if you can't lock him up, join him. Hence, we often make date weekends out of my husband's business trips.

The most significant consolations of business travel are the frequent flyer, car rental, and hotel programs. We often redeem my husband's mileage points for my airline ticket, and we redeem hotel points for weekend stays. All he needs to do is feed me. He also saves money by staying over Saturday night instead of traveling home on Friday.

While my husband is working on these business trips, I have a perfect opportunity to relax and get ready for our time together. I always bring a book that I am anxious to read. And I catch up on correspondence, take naps, sun bathe, and even visit some sights that only I would enjoy. Then when my husband returns, I am ready to give him my complete attention.

It is definitely a challenge to make the necessary arrangements to pull off such a getaway. I have children to care for, and I have my own employer to keep happy. So I need to be creative.

I use grandparents whenever possible, and I have exchanged babysitting with my friends, watching their children when they want to get away. I explained my situation to my employer and worked out an arrangement that meets both our needs. I put in extra hours to cover the days I might miss and often take work home so that I can finish all my work. I also try to coordinate my trips with the slower seasons so that my boss isn't put out by me being gone.

The best part of traveling with my husband is having the opportunity to share in the things that couples ordinarily share together at home. We dine together, discuss ideas, pray together, kiss each other good night, and cuddle in the morning. When we spend time together in this way, our marital life is complete. These trips are an enjoyable and worthwhile investment in our relationship. And it's a great way to beat the "travelin' man blues!"

Ken and Kendra Davis
Married June 5, 1999

With today's busy work environment, it is not unusual for a husband or a wife to travel frequently for business. This poses a difficult situation in many marriages. Oftentimes, complaining and fighting can become the norm, not affection and connection.

Times like these call for extreme measures. This couple refused to fall prey to the stresses caused by a traveling mate. Instead, this husband and wife made their own rules. It took some creativity and special arrangements, but it paid off.

It might take time and effort but if work schedules make connecting with your spouse difficult, try something different. Tag along on a business trip once in a while. Just the plane flight alone can be a special time of uninterrupted conversation.

Schedules today demand that we reach outside the box and come up with any way possible to bring connection into our marriages. Maybe this couple's idea can work for you.
Why not give it a try?
It might change your marriage.

A Sitter's Guide

Once you have children, an important thing to do is find a sitter. This isn't as hard as you think. There are resources everywhere. Try asking your local church or nearby school for a list. Your friends are a great resource as well. If you can develop a list of several available sitters that both spouses have on hand, you will be set for any date.

The following tips will help life with your sitter go more smoothly:

- Create a list of emergency numbers and include a neighbor or other local contact. Include your address and cell phone numbers as well.

- Make sure you have a predetermined bedtime that has been clearly stated for everyone. This will make bedtime easier for the sitter. If you leave bedtime open-ended, you may find the kids still up when you get home. Review any bedtime routines with everyone; i.e. bath time, special reading books, etc. This will give the sitter more chance for success in getting your kids to bed on time.

- Splurge and get some fun videos and a special dessert or snack for the kids and the sitter. This will make them feel good about your going out. Make this something you wouldn't do if you were home so the kids will think your dates are a treat for them as well.

- Predetermine how late your sitter can stay and adhere to that time. Be home when you say you will be home. You put a sitter in a difficult situation when you call and ask them to stay out later than you have arranged. If you are unreliable, your sitter will not want to return.

- Moms should take female babysitters home, and dads should take male babysitters home. This is for everyone's safety and protection.

Finding the right babysitter will make everything easier when you finally get the opportunity to have some special time for yourselves.

Don't neglect getting a sitter; it is not an option, but a must. Make dating a priority for your marriage. You will never regret it.

62

Ten
Bubble Memories

Each year on our anniversary we try to go somewhere different and do something new to keep the fire burning and give us fresh memories. About nine years ago, one of these anniversary trips exceeded our expectations in the memory department.

I made reservations to take my wife to a little hotel on the beach in the central coast of California. I splurged and requested a special room with a Jacuzzi. On our way to the hotel, we stopped in a little Dutch tourist town to do some shopping. While my wife eyed some cute little antiques, I stole away to a candle store and stocked up on scented candles and bubble bath.

We arrived that evening at the hotel, and my wife was very impressed with all the arrangements, especially the tub! As she got herself ready for a dip in the tub, I placed the candles around the room and added some bubble bath to the Jacuzzi. I filled the tub with the right temperature water and set the timer for the jets. As we climbed in, I was very disappointed in the amount of bubbles being produced, so I grabbed the bubble bath and added some more—a lot more! I lit the candles just in time for the jets to turn on. We were ready for an evening of romance.

Then it happened. As the jets fired up, so did the bubble bath. Before we knew it, I couldn't see my wife anymore on the other side of the tub. The bubbles kept coming and began to spill over the edge of the tub! The last thing we needed was for the bubbles to begin seeping out our door.

In our birthday suits, we started scooping up bubbles and dumping them into the regular tub that was also in the bathroom. No matter how hard or how fast we worked, we never seemed to get ahead. The bubbles were definitely winning. By the time we got things under control, we had a mountain of bubbles in the regular bathtub, the sink, and the toilet! All the while we were laughing so hard the neighbors must have been wondering what we were doing.

We finally made it back into the Jacuzzi, red-faced and with aching stomachs from laughing so hard. My best intentions toward romance had taken a huge belly flop! But we do have a memory that we will never forget. And if we ever need a laugh, we just return to that cute little hotel room on the beach with a Jacuzzi.

Gary and Sue Becker
Married April 28, 1973

When was the last time you
laughed together?

Nothing breaks the ice more in a relationship than laughter. You
know the kind—when you laugh so much your stomach hurts!

Sometimes you can plan things to a tee,
and they just go haywire.
Don't let this ruin a date. Laugh!
This might be the memory you could
never have planned.
Thank God for giving you this special opportunity to experience a
moment of real joy together.

Unfortunately, these moments are
few and far between.
When you are gifted with a moment of laughter
together, rejoice and run with it.
It may have to last you far too long.
Cherish those times when a moment of chuckling can make a connection that will last forever.

Eleven
Cupid Has Arrived

One particular Valentine's Day gave me a new definition for the word romance.

The day turned out to be rainy and dreary. We had made plans for a nice, typical Valentine's Day date, but I threw a ringer into the plans when I came down with a nasty cold. My husband, Tom, was very accommodating and suggested we just stay home and cuddle on the sofa, wrapped together in blankets.

About 6:30 or so that evening, Tom got up and said he needed to go out to get something. I didn't think much of it; I just assumed he was going to the store to get something to eat. About a half an hour later, the doorbell rang, and I got up to see who it was. When I opened the door, there was Tom, standing with nothing on but a homemade diaper, holding a bow and an arrow, and shouting, "Happy Valentine's Day." It was Cupid himself! Behind him stood a lady with a catered dinner for the two of us!

What a nice surprise! But the best surprise was soon to come. After he greeted me with a warm "Happy Valentine's Day" hug, he wiggled just a little too much and his diaper fell completely off, leaving him standing in his underwear in the hallway. We all laughed so hard. It was truly a Kodak moment and one that still brings us laughter today. I loved his creativity and his desire to make it a really special, intimate evening.

Tom and Martha McCall
Married October 20, 1984

Have you lost your spontaneity?

When was the last time you tried something on a whim?
Many of us have lost the desire to be creative or to be impulsive.
Yet it is these moments that can often bring us the
greatest joy and longest lasting memories.
Sometimes we can laugh over those spontaneous
moments for years to come.

We are so creative about bringing fun into the lives of our children.
Why not try something outlandish on a date with your spouse?
You don't have to don a diaper, but you could put your inhibitions
aside and live life on the wild side for one night.

Think of the fun you will have as you surprise your
mate with your wacky idea.
It could be just the spark your marriage needs to
get the flame roaring again.

Top 10
Things Not to Say on a Date

10 "Have you ever thought about how much money we would have if we didn't have kids?"

9 "How long has it been since you colored your hair?"

8 "It's almost 9:00 p.m. and we don't want to miss the end of the big game."

7 "Do you think I am getting fat?"

6 "Do you think the kids are O.K.?"

5 "May I have extra garlic, please?"

4 "I think I forgot to put on my deodorant."

3 "When are you going to get a job that pays more money?"

2 "That's a little expensive."

1 "I need to get back to work."

Twelve
our Night In

Once our fourth child was born, going out on a "real" date became nearly impossible. It was hard enough finding a sitter for two or three children, but now we had a fourth little one. We couldn't find anyone whom we felt could handle the load. Also, the cost of a sitter for this crew was out of our range. We needed to keep within the budget of our now six-member family.

It wasn't long before connecting became a distant thought as my husband and I became immersed in the drudgeries of having a house full of little children. Romance—what was that?

We knew we had to come up with some way to connect in our marriage before things got out of control. What could we do on our limited budget with a brood always in the house with us? In desperation we came up with an idea—an "at-home date." We decided to pick Tuesday evening as the night we would have a date at home. We chose this time to plan a gourmet meal that we could later prepare and enjoy together.

Needless to say, this took a little planning and preparation time. First, we picked the meal and purchased all the ingredients ahead of time. Then came the real work. We fed the kids and took care of all baths and pre-bed details early. Then we had the kids read or watch a special video. (Our ten-year-old was always a special help with the baby.) Finally, we began to prepare our special meal.

By the time we starting cooking in the kitchen, it was close to bedtime for all the children. When it came time to serve our meal, we settled the children in bed and made sure the dining room was decorated nicely with candles, often with some mood music playing in the background. Frequently we even pulled out the nice china. Then it was our time to enjoy a delicious meal alone! We spent time talking and catching up from the week and generally reconnecting.

After dinner we often watched a rented movie together or challenged each other to a viscous card game. Whatever the activity, we enjoyed what had become a special night for us— our "at-home date" night. This was definitely just what we needed to get us through those years with so many little ones at home and to keep the romance burning.

Joey and Krista O'Connor
Married May 13, 1989

It is a wonderful time of life—
that time when the children are young.
and each day brings a new adventure.
But it can be a tough time for a marriage.
Getting together for quality romantic
time can be difficult.

This couple didn't let a house full
of children and tight finances keep them from connecting. They dug down deep and came up with a plan that
gave them some much needed time together.

You can't be all you can be for your
children until you make your marriage
the priority it needs to be.
If you are in the stage of life when
children fill your world, find a time for connection in your
marriage, even
if it means having a special date
at home once a week.
It will be the best gift you could
ever give to your children.

When It's O.K. to Date at Home

Whenever possible, try to create dates that
force the two of you out the front door.
However, there are times when it just can't be done.
Maybe there are too many young children to attend to.

Sometimes finances can't accommodate a date
out on the town.
Perhaps getting it all together to go out is
just too overwhelming.

If you find yourself at a time in your life when going out on
a date doesn't work for you, don't stop dating.
Go ahead and prepare for a date at home.
Plan a special moment for the two of you in the living room,
the kitchen, or even the bedroom.

It is O.K. for you to have a date at home … sometimes.

SWEETHEART, YOU ARE AMAZING! THAT DRESS,
THIS MEAL, ALL THESE DECORATIONS!
SO WHAT DID YOU DO WITH THE BABY?

75

Thirteen
Antique Love

As Mark and I loaded our daughters' sleeping bags and suitcases into the car, I began thinking about their week away at camp. This would be the first week they were both away, leaving us at home alone.

During the hour drive, our girls talked excitedly about camp—cabinmates and food fears. I wondered if our nine year old would really be able to handle a whole week on her own. I gently reminded her to please change her clothes at least once.

After arriving at the camp, we settled the girls into their cabins and said our long good-byes. As Mark and I headed back to the car, without our sweet daughters, I found comfort in the hand of my husband. I knew that I would be putting my maternal instincts on hold for a week (except for daily letters and two care packages), but I knew this one-on-one time with my husband was important too. I began to look forward to our time together.

We had driven only ten miles, and I was already feeling as if we had left our girls in a different country, when Mark pulled off the road into the parking lot of an antique store I had spotted on our way to the camp. Mark looked at me with a sweet, tender look in his eye, knowing that if anything could make this mother in mourning feel better, it would be a stroll through an antique shop! I've always enjoyed antiques; Mark has never particularly cared for them. I wouldn't have asked him to stop, but his stopping meant everything to me. The hour we spent combing over the antiques kicked off our week of enjoying each other in a time-extravagant way.

When I think of all the dinner reservations we've made, all the movies we've watched, all the trips we've shared, that spontaneous antique shop date is still one of the most memorable moments in our fourteen years of marriage. I learned that nothing feels better than having my interests acknowledged and indulged. Mark may not care for antiques, but he loves a woman who does.

I could go on and on about how wonderful that afternoon was to me, but I have a football game to watch.

Mark and Kelly Schwartz
Married January 10, 1987

Do you indulge your spouse's
interests and desires?

Or do you find them too mundane and
trite to acknowledge?
When was the last time you made the effort to recognize
the needs of your mate and then try to fulfill them?

This husband knew his wife and knew what she was feeling
on this particular day.
He made the effort to get her through a difficult time by
making her feel important.
He sacrificed his own desires
to meet hers.

Whether it's shopping for antiques or spending time looking at tools in the local hardware store, time encouraging
each other's interests can make lasting memories.
Take time to learn about what brings joy
to your mate and then participate
in that joy with them.

You never know, it may open up a whole new world to you.

SEE? ISN'T THIS MORE FUN THAN "ANTIQUING"?

Fourteen
Protecting Our Time

As our children enter their late teens, my husband and I look back on the childhood years with great affection. Although we didn't always have the funds to go out on any date we desired, at least the kids were on a schedule that allowed us the ability to dictate just how much of our time they could lay claim to.

Now it isn't uncommon for us to have a day that begins at 5 a.m. and ends at midnight, not due to our schedule, but due to the schedule of our busy preadult children. Now that we can no longer set their bedtime at 8 p.m., the private time that my husband and I used to cherish has become a distant memory.

So how do we stay connected? Well, it takes work. More than we thought it would. We used to struggle to find sitters in order to sneak out to a simple movie, now we have to make use of each and every moment we have to be alone. One thing that has become special to us as a couple is for my husband to stay home a little later a few mornings a week so that when the kids head off to school or work at 7 a.m., we can have a private breakfast together. It may be at home, sharing a cup of coffee over the kitchen table, or once in a while at our favorite breakfast spot in town. Wherever it may be, this has become an intimate moment for us to connect.

One advantage to having older kids is that you can leave them alone. This has allowed us to take a few overnight escapes. The most memorable was on my husband's last birthday. I took the time to plan the getaway and reserved a room at a local bed-and-breakfast. I packed a bag for my husband and when he arrived home from work, I whisked him away for a simple overnight stay without all the pressures and commitments of home. Although we needed to be home for one of the kids' many events at 9 a.m. the next day, it was just what we needed to remind ourselves that we really still liked each other.

As our children have gotten older, I have begun to allow them the opportunity to become more financially responsible for some of their many needs, i.e. sports equipment, music, clothing. This has given my husband and me the ability to do a little more for each other financially. It was amazing to me how I wouldn't flinch at dropping $100 on our son for his latest sporting needs, yet when it came to my husband, I would become a grinch! Now I realize the importance of drawing the line with my children in order to be able to splurge a little on my husband.

Ann and Len Svenson
Married August 29, 1975

Are you at this point in your marriage when the kids'
schedules have taken over your life? Many of us know
what this is like. It can be all consuming!

Be different.
Pick a time that works
for you and go with it.
It may not be Friday date night, it may be an impromptu
lunch or one of those two-hour breakfasts when you
pour over the paper together once a week.
Remember those days of old?

Don't feel as if you have to fit into
the mold of what
others say a date has to be.
Make your dates special for you and
your mate alone.

MAYBE WE'D STAND A BETTER CHANCE OF SPICING
UP OUR MARRIAGE IF WE *AVOIDED* THESE INTIMATE
EARLY MORNING RENDEVOUS

Fifteen
Do I Know You?

Tony and I had known each other for seven years before we decided to "tie the knot" in November 1986. Another four years passed before our daughter Erika was born in November 1990.

As a well-scheduled business couple, we were diligent in blocking out time for our weekly date night with each other after Erika was born. Our dates were extremely romantic, spontaneous, and rich with deep conversation. We varied our nights out either by going to dinner and a show or going to dinner and a show or going to dinner and a show.

By the time our eighth wedding anniversary rolled around, we had seen just about every movie out there and tried every restaurant in Orange County. We had officially transitioned from the "romantic" stage of marriage to the "comfortable, complacent, couch potato" stage.

DATES FOR MATES

At work, Tony had been conducting financial advisory seminars for real estate professionals. Many of his individual appointments were with people from that field, seeking investment and financial direction.

One day a Ms. Stacy Jones called to schedule an appointment with Tony. She was an extremely successful real estate professional from out-of-state who had attended one of my husband's seminars. When she called to schedule her appointment, she informed my husband's secretary that she would be flying into Orange County for a brief visit. Her schedule would be very busy; therefore, she only had about forty-five minutes to meet Tony and get advice as to how she should prudently invest the $500,000 that she had accumulated. Since time was of the essence, she arranged to meet my husband in the lobby of the hotel where she was staying while in town.

According to my husband's secretary, he was a little put off that this woman couldn't take the time to meet him in his office as other professionals did, but he finally agreed to meet her at her hotel. Tony was advised that Ms. Jones would be wearing a large black hat and that he should have no trouble spotting her in the lobby.

When my husband entered the lobby, it didn't take him long to spot Stacy Jones and her large black hat. As he approached her,she was looking down and reading over some documents so he had to bend down, peak under the hat, and call her name all at the same time in order to make the initial introduction.

I will never forget the look of shock, disorientation, speechlessness, and surprise on my husband's face when I looked up at him from under that hat. As he was trying to recover, I said, "Happy Anniversary!" Then I ushered him up to the hotel room I had booked for the weekend. Needless to say, we didn't go out for dinner and a show that weekend. We spent our time rekindling that romantic fire that had gone out in our relationship. Our special evening reminded us why we loved each other so much.

Tony and Carin Amaradio
Married November 1, 1986

Have your dates become stale?

Maybe you end up doing the same
thing every time you go out.
Sure, dinner and a movie sound great.
It doesn't take too much thought,
but it works.

Often we are so busy and stressed from life, that to be creative takes more than we have to give. But once in a while,
we need to break out of the routine and
try something different.

A unique date can rekindle the flame that brought you
both together in the beginning.
But it seldom happens by accident.

Take the time to plan a different date,
one that stretches your imagination.
It may take time and a little extra effort and planning, but
the payoff is well worth it.

Why not think of something new today?

You Look Marvelous

Sloppy.
That's part of the problem.
We've gotten sloppy.
Oh, sure, you make the effort to
look nice for other people.
But what about looking nice for your mate?
It's understandable.
Your spouse lives with you.
It is your down time.
You don't want to bother
impressing anymore.

But just remember.
The more attractive you make yourself look,
the more interested your spouse becomes.
See what kind of response you get the next
time you put forth that extra effort.
Pull out the cologne, press the clothes,
and add a little "spit and polish."

What happens may surprise you.

sixteen
Strength for the storm

Our son, Drew, was diagnosed with a heart condition at six weeks of age, which led immediately to his first surgery at seven weeks. Now he is ten and has faced five operations, three of which involved open-heart surgery.

Drew's health situation has presented us with special challenges in our dating life. It became clear to us early on that we were going to have to take close notice of our marriage because we saw a life of ups and downs ahead of us. It isn't easy to leave any child at home with a sitter, but leaving a child with special needs is almost impossible. Our son's care and needs demanded more than a local babysitter could handle.

Thankfully, my loving brother and sister-in-law took a special interest in our situation and in us. When Drew was young, they learned how to care for him, including his quirks and special needs. They took the time to learn about all of his medicines and which red flags to watch for. Then they went one step further and offered to take care of Drew sometimes so that my husband and I could have some special time of reconnection. Little did they know what an impact these times made in our lives!

Not very long ago, we received one of their wonderful invitations to take Drew for an overnighter so that we could spend some time alone in San Diego. We dropped our son off and headed out on our little adventure. It was so nice to have time to talk about the fun times in our lives and to reconnect. We dined out, had massages, and played golf.

When we returned home, we felt refreshed and renewed. No one had any idea how timely this getaway would prove to be. The following Monday we faced a new health challenge as tests revealed an urgent need for our son to face yet another surgery. Another long road lay ahead of us.

Without that time away, I'm not sure how well we would be facing this new challenge in our lives. I can never begin to thank my brother and his wife for giving us the wonderful gift of time—time together. It has given us the strength to get through the tough times and still remain committed to each other.

Ed and Roxanne Nilsen
Married August 27, 1983

Does your marriage bear a special burden?
It could be an ill child or an aging parent.
But caring for another brings its
own unique challenges.
Sometimes these burdens can put more weight
on a marriage than it can bear.

If your marriage is feeling stretched in this way—reach out.
Find a family member or friend you can trust to help you. Don't try
to make it alone.
Try connecting with a couple in the same situation and trade date
times. Their marriage needs this, too.

And if you aren't in this situation but know
a couple who is, reach out and
offer to help them.

Plan a special evening or moment for the two of them.
Make the reservations, arrange the details,
and even hire the sitter.
Maybe you could take the kids for an overnighter.
Let their time together be a reminder of
how much they really mean to each other.

It may be the most precious gift
you could ever give them.

SHE SLEEPS BEST IF YOU RUN THE VACUUM
AND HER FAVORITE GAMES ARE WATCHING
SOME ONE DUST OR FOLD LAUNDRY

Seventeen

Romance after Twins

Starting to date again after having a child is hard. But starting to date after having twins is a challenge! My husband, Lew, and I had only been married a year when the twins came into our lives. It was quite a shock to our marriage. We had hardly enjoyed the benefits of being newlyweds when we were immediately thrown into the completely new world of parenthood with no concept of what to do.

Although I was exhausted and stretched to my limit most of the time, I tried to be open to any way possible to connect with Lew. I would try to plan lunch dates when the girls were sleeping or be open to attending the evening events for his company. Yet invariably, the girls would fight the nap or throw up on my evening dress just as we were ready to leave for the night!

DATES FOR MATES

One night Lew and I decided that we would get the girls to bed early and have a romantic evening at home. I bought steaks and all the ingredients for his favorite meal and made sure everything was set in the dining room. I pulled out a special negligee, making sure it still fit, and dusted off that particular bottle of perfume that got Lew's juices flowing. His job was to get the girls settled in bed while I headed off to wait for him in the shower.

After several minutes alone in the shower, I began to wonder what was holding up my husband. It wasn't long before the nice warm water began to turn chilly. I headed out to see what was causing the delay. As I turned the corner, there was my husband, in his underwear, running around trying to clean up after one of the twins who had thrown up in her bed.

He was trying desperately to accomplish this goal before I found out because he knew that the romance he was seeking would promptly be shoved aside for the sake of motherhood. No such luck. Immediately, twin number two soon joined her sister by throwing up all over her bed. We spent the next few hours washing sheets, giving baths, and rocking babies back to sleep. By the time it was over, we were exhausted.

Yet, there was a somewhat happy ending. We did finally make it into the shower. (We needed one in order to get rid of that smell!) And we did enjoy a nice dinner. But once again our sweet little angels had thwarted our best efforts for romance.

We didn't give up on dating, however. After fifteen years of marriage and four children, we have made every effort to protect that time set aside just for us. It has proved to be the saving grace of our marriage and has provided a wonderful example of a loving relationship to our precious daughters.

Lew and Laura Webb
Married November 2, 1985

A new baby can change your life in
more ways than you ever expect.
It can throw your marriage into
a complete tizzy!
Dating after a baby is a challenge,
but one that you must face head on.
Make that time together as husband
and wife a priority, no matter
how hard it may seem.
Remember that without your marriage, that one you hold
so precious and dear would not be here for you to love.
If at first you don't succeed, try, try again.
This couple didn't give up because of
one evening of discouragement.
They kept trying and made dating an important part of
their family life.
And along the way, they set an example
for their children of what it means
to cherish a marriage.
The time to make the connection is now—before it gets
away from you or something else takes its place.

IF I DIDN'T KNOW BETTER I'D THINK YOU GUYS
WERE LOOKING _FORWARD_ TO US GOING TO BED

Dating on Purpose

"Hey look! We had two dates last month,
and it was no big deal!"
"Yeah right!"

Couples the world over love the idea
of passionate nights, shared adventures,
and romantic memories.
However, the dates that facilitate those
moments don't happen by accident.
They are the products of thoughtful
decisions made by people who
make their marriage a priority.

Sooner or later you have to put books
like this one down and go out on
that much needed date.
That is, unless you want everyone else
to have all the fun.

Eighteen
December In Hartford

I can imagine it is rare for both partners in a marriage to have the same perspective on a particular meaningful moment in their relationship. What may have been significant to one may be quickly forgotten by the other.

However, neither my wife nor I will ever forget December 1995. Debbie and I staggered into the Christmas season, tired after nineteen years of holding a marriage together that had been bursting at the seams. A year or so earlier, we had come to grips with commitment issues and this forced us to renew our efforts to rebuild our relationship. But with the real time demands of family life and financial pressures, combined with the weariness of a long marriage journey, I think our progress was slower than we had hoped.

DATES FOR MATES

As December approached, a friend and business associate invited me to Connecticut for a day of meetings during the Christmas season. "Bring your wife along," he suggested. "I want to treat the two of you to a weekend at a very special bed and breakfast about ninety miles outside Hartford."

Debbie and I hadn't been away together for sixteen years, since we started having kids. We talked about it and decided to make the trip. The extra plane ticket was a bit of a stretch, but we went anyway.

It's funny. I don't remember a lot about our wedding, our honeymoon, or other "special events" we have shared over the lifetime of our marriage. But I do remember almost every single moment about those two December days in Hartford.

I remember watching the snow out the window as our plane slowly taxied toward the airport in Hartford. I remember hearing the flight attendant say our plane was the last one allowed to land that evening because of the snowstorm. I remember standing in line to get the last rental car and shuffling outside through the falling snowflakes to get to our car.

I remember looking over in the darkness and watching Debbie try to read my friend's directions to our overnight lodging. I remember our initial panic because his instructions took us off the main highway and had us plodding through backwoods, softly illuminated by a full moon and lily-white falling snow. I remember rolling down our windows and listening to our tires crunching on the fresh snow as we inched our way along, the only car on a single-lane, wooded road.

I remember rounding a curve and seeing just ahead a solitary antique store, hidden back in those quiet parts, the smoke spiraling out its chimney on that snowy night. For some reason it was still open at that late hour—it was after nine. We pulled up and ran inside to use the bathroom. I remember we stayed an hour, walking among the antiques, drinking hot cider, and whispering to each other so as not to draw attention to ourselves. We had departed Earth and had landed on Pluto. Our problems seemed a universe away.

I remember getting back into the car and finally making our way to our bed and breakfast. I remember walking in, being greeted by name, and smelling Christmas in the air. I also remember panicking because there was no television in the room.

We spent two days in that inn that December weekend. I remember it as the beginning of the second half of our marriage. It reminded us that we were still people who enjoyed each other, and that there was life after kids and all the other stuff. And it encouraged us to take time for ourselves, reminding us that we were first a couple and then a mom and dad.

I love December now. Connecticut is my favorite state. My house is full of antiques. And we are on year twenty-five.

It's funny what a good weekend can do.

Thom and Debbie Black
Married June 5, 1976

There are certain events create a memory only you and your mate can share—one so private and special that no one else can even understand.

Has it been too long since you and your mate created a memory?
Do you even remember the last time you had a moment together that made an imprint that no one could erase?

Times like these deliver us into another world.
A world far from the stresses and demands of our everyday lives.
A world where we can rediscover each other and begin again.

Why not make a memory?
Take the time to plan something special that only you and your mate will understand.
It might just be the beginning of something new for your marriage.

Ahh ... memories.

ON _YOUR_ DREAM DATE I SAT IN A TREE
IN THE POURING RAIN WEARING CAMOUFLAGE
AND DABBING DEER URINE BEHIND MY EARS.
NOW QUIT WHINING AND PADDLE.

Nineteen
That Newlywed Feeling

It's amazing how life gets away from us. We get busy with our jobs, start having kids, buy a house, become involved in school and church activities, and poof! No more time for us.

For Steve and I, the area we felt got "squeezed" the most was our physical relationship. Our times alone had become stale and predictable. I felt as if we were starting to act old. But I didn't feel old!

By this time it was our children who were getting older. One was in college and the other two were in high school. So it was a little easier to get away now than it had been in years past. We decided to make an overnight date to a place called "The Sybaris," a romantic motel with some very distinguishing features. We planned ahead by bringing a picnic dinner to eat in our room. We thought of romantic foods—shrimp, vegetables and dip, cheese and bread, fruit, and finally, cheesecake. We even planned for the next day's breakfast with bagels and cream cheese and some juice.

When we arrived, we were surprised by the wonderful array of romantic features the room had to offer. It was equipped with a king size bed, a big screen TV, a wonderful sound system, our own sauna room, and the most fun of all, our own individual pool right in our room.

Our date began in that room, and we didn't leave until we went home the next day. We were exhausted. Our kids pestered us all the next week, wanting to hear what we did all weekend. They just couldn't imagine how we had spent all that time. Some day they will figure it out.

That weekend was so meaningful to us because it reminded us how important the physical side of our relationship is to the intimacy and vulnerability we desired between us. What seemed like a silly idea turned out to be an important building block in our marriage.

Steve and Chris Rogers
Married May 8, 1974

Isn't it amazing how the physical intimacy in marriage is the first thing we put aside and the last thing to get our attention?
Isn't this what we couldn't get enough of when we first got married?

Who has time to be intimate anymore?
Between the career, the kids, the laundry—who has the energy?

If your marriage needs a boost, why not book some time for sheer romance?
Let it be a time that takes you back to being newlyweds.

And if you can't get away, try the little things.
Give each other private little touches in the kitchen and steal passionate kisses in the hallway.
Don't let a day go by when you don't take the time to nurture this most neglected area of marriage.

WELL, THE KIDS ARE FINALLY ALL GONE.
NOW WHAT WAS IT WE WANTED TO DO?

Twenty

Something out of Nothing

It was Valentine's Day, 1991. I was almost two weeks late with our first baby. I had just started maternity leave and was waiting anxiously for this baby to be born. I was one of those pregnant women who carried the baby all the way out in front so I looked like a beached whale, and now I was starting to feel like one.

Mark and I were planning to go out to dinner to celebrate the holiday since this was probably going to be one of our last dates as a carefree couple. Our lives had become very busy with our careers and outside commitments. We had been scrambling to find time to connect and prepare for this new phase of our lives. Not very successfully, I might note. This Valentine's Day evening was going to be an important time for us.

It must have started snowing sometime in the afternoon. Outside everything was quickly becoming blanketed in a covering of white. Invariably whenever we would have special plans, something would come up to spoil them. So, of course, tonight was no exception. It wasn't long before Mark called to say he would be late; however, he did promised we would still have our date.

The afternoon dragged into the evening, and the snow showed no signs of letting up. Repeated trips to the window confirmed that I was still alone. About 8:00 p.m. the phone rang. It was Mark. He was calling from a pay phone next to the tollbooth on the highway (before the days of cell phones). "Yes, I am still alive," he said. "I have been stuck in traffic for three hours. Do you still want to go out for dinner?"

Now let me make this clear. It's Valentine's Day, maybe the busiest night of the year for dinner. We now have no dinner reservations, and I am a starving, pregnant whale who can't go more than a couple of hours without being fed. My husband is more than a couple of miles from home in a full-blown snowstorm. In answer to Mark's question, I said: "No, I don't think so. Pick up some hot dogs on the way home."

While I was waiting for Mark to come home, I decided to stop feeling sorry for myself. I got out the candles, set a romantic table, and put Kenny G on the stereo. Mark came staggering in about an hour later, hot dogs in one hand and wilted flowers he had bought twelve hours earlier in the other.

In the quietness of a broken-down evening, over candlelight and hot dogs, two very busy people talked for the first time about some of the changes they would face in the days ahead. We talked about what it would mean to be a mom and a dad, what we felt about it, and how frightened each of us really was. We talked about the early days of our marriage, and we laughed a lot. I think most of all, we discovered each other again that night.

It's funny. We have been married ten years. We have three children. Over the years we have been on countless trips and adventures together. But none of them holds a place in my heart like that one, quiet evening, apart from the lights and the crowds, when my husband and I rediscovered our love.

Denise and Mark Hartman
Married February 8, 1990

Sometimes we need to improvise.

Often, our best-laid plans fall quickly by the wayside. If we stick with great rigidity to the plan and refuse to be flexible, we can destroy a moment.

How often we make plans only to have something beyond our control mess them up.
Maybe it is a last-minute project causing you to stay late at work, or maybe it is a child who picked your special moment to come down with the flu.

Who would have known this couple's plan for romance would be thwarted by a snowstorm? Thank goodness they chose to be open to the moment and allowed something to come from nothing. This became a moment they could never replace.

Choose to be open to a night of improvising.
You never know what blessing it may bring.

ARE YOU SURE YOU WOULDN'T RATHER COOK?

Twenty-One
Seeing with New Eyes

I have six kids, all under the age of twelve. You can imagine all the time I spend doing laundry, cooking meals, cleaning, and playing chauffeur. It is nonstop. In addition, I am the at-home bookkeeper and secretary for my husband's production company. The reality of my life is that I never get time for myself, much less time with my spouse.

But I love it all. I love being needed. I love the responsibility. I love the kids, and most of all I love my husband. We are singularly committed to each other, and I think knowing that has allowed us to focus on other areas of need for all these years. For twelve years, Danny and I have never found the time to take even one evening away for ourselves.

I don't know how that happened, but it did. Since we

seemed to be doing fine, we didn't pay much attention to it. Every once in a while one of us would bring it up, but finding sitters and scheduling a time to get away together around all the kids' stuff was just too complicated. Besides, I would miss the kids even if we were away for an evening.

My parents, in all their wisdom, decided to get us moving. For our fifteenth wedding anniversary, they gave us a trip to Hawaii. We were excited, yet I was petrified. There was no way we could possibly do this. We couldn't take off for a single evening. How were we supposed to leave for a week? If it weren't so ridiculous, it would be funny.

Nevertheless, Danny and I made reservations to make my parents happy. We made sure the reservations were far enough in the future (ten months away) that we wouldn't have to think about it. Suddenly, the day was on top of us. My parents were coming to stay with the kids, so all of the family routines would stay intact; however, I was grieving. The month before we left, I felt as if someone was dying. I was more worried that I wouldn't make it than that the kids would have a hard time. My life had become my children.

I called home twice on the cell phone on the way to the airport. I was leaving my six kids! Didn't anyone care how miserable I was?

When we landed in Hawaii, everything was as beautiful as it could be. Still I couldn't shake my feeling of emptiness. I wanted my children to be here, too.

On our first morning in paradise, Danny and I went off the island to snorkel. Neither of us had ever snorkeled, and we didn't know what to expect. It simply was one of the most beautiful experiences of my life. Danny and I floated in water as clear as glass, our arms spread wide while all manner of spectacular sea life swam around us. We felt like children ourselves as we experienced an intimacy that was new to both of us, larger than either of us. We knew what was happening was important to us both, and we struggled for words to share with each other what we were feeling.

It was such a meaningful time for us. We were outside of our day-to-day routine, sharing something together that redefined us individually and as a couple. I had been so busy these last twelve years that I had forgotten how glorious the world around me was and I was rediscovering it with my husband.

Don't get me wrong. I still missed the kids. And we still don't get out as much as we should. But something happened to us on that date to Hawaii that changed us forever.

I can't wait to take the children.

Danny and Lori Richards
Married January 5, 1985

Marriage is one of the greatest gifts
we could ever have been given.
Yet how often we put everything else
ahead of it.
We allow work, children, hobbies, sports,
anything else to take us away from
what truly matters.

Thank goodness for wise parents and friends
who intercede and force us to look at
things in a different way.
Do you have people like this in your life?
Maybe you should listen to them.
They may have a clearer viewpoint than you do.

This couple had a moment of renewal they
didn't even know they needed.
They may have gone kicking and screaming,
but they returned with a new perspective
about each other and their marriage.

If you have an opportunity to
break out of the routine and recapture those
feelings of old, take it.
Don't allow anything to hold you back
or get in the way.

Treat Your Spouse As Well As You Treat Your Children

Did you ever believe you would hear someone saying this?

But in all honesty, don't we treat our kids better than we treat our spouse?

We pay close attention to all our kids say and do, we volunteer and get involved in their activities, we encourage them, love them, and know just what they need when they've had a bad day.

All week long we exhaust ourselves attending to our children, and neglect the very person who helped bring them into our life?

Be aware of how you treat your mate during the week. Try giving him or her the same love and respect you lavish on your children.

You might find your marriage will be more fun.

Twenty-Two
Somewhere in Time

We have a few movies that we love to watch as a couple. Movies that seem to be so romantic. One of them is "Somewhere in Time," the story of a man who goes back in time to find a woman he had discovered in an old photograph. He finds her, actually falls in love with her, but then mistakenly returns to his own time, leaving his love lost forever in the past. The movie haunts us both.

The movie takes place in The Grand Hotel on Mackinac Island, a glorious, turn of the century hotel on a very small island in Lake Michigan. Visitors to the island must reach it by ferry and leave their cars behind.

My husband and I decided to capture our own magic after watching the movie for the third or fourth time. We made reservations for a long weekend and agreed to pack separate boxes that would contain some of the special memories of our early days together. We got sitters for the kids and made the seven-hour drive; excited to experience firsthand the beauty of this island for ourselves.

As the taxi door swung open, we could feel the emotions of a man and woman longing for a lost love. Walking up the long, winding drive to The Grand Hotel, we felt as if somehow we had been transported into the movie itself.

We checked in at the magnificent front desk we had seen many times on our VCR, and we received our room—perhaps the very one in which the two lovers first met.

After an early dinner, we returned to our room and began to share the items we had packed in our memory boxes. We spent an hour looking at old yearbooks and photographs that had been hidden away for years. We took out old gifts and funny clothes we had worn when we were dating. Then we both pulled out a stack of love letters from each other that we had saved. Neither knew the other still had such letters.

One at a time, we took turns reading them to each other. Could we have written these words? Was it true that at one time we had been the center of each other's universe? What beautiful thoughts, what beautiful love, hidden for all this time. Precious words on quiet pieces of paper.

Every year my husband and I go back to The Grand Hotel. Before we leave to come home, we write to each other expressions of love that remain sealed away until the following year, to be read as reminders of the love that brought us here. Our past, we have discovered, is the most important part of our relationship, hidden back there, somewhere in time.

Cliff and Tanya Burke
Married September 23, 1977

Isn't it amazing how fast time flies?

Before you know it, years have passed by without notice.
What memories from your past have gotten lost and
need to recapture?
Maybe it's a love that burned so brightly that nothing else
mattered but being together.

Wouldn't it be great to live a fantasy life
for just a short time?
To pretend that you were in another place or time for
even just a moment? Maybe a getaway to a historic hotel
or restaurant might be just the ticket.
Or perhaps something as simple as spending time remi-
niscing over old photographs of your early years together.

Whatever you choose as your "fantasy" trip, make it memorable. Take the time to be alone and to remember those
special times together.
Recapture those memories and create
new ones in the process.
Remind yourselves about that burning love of years past.

Same Date—Different Year

Perhaps the most treasured of all dates is the date you
celebrate on the same day each year.

It's a date that provides romance, memories, tradition,
significance, and a backdrop to an evolving relationship.
It offers an escape that calls out to you
months before it actually arrives.
It reminds you of the best parts of your marriage
together.

The commitment you make to set a this time aside each
year is a priceless reminder of the commitment you
have made to each other in your marriage.

Have some fun picking the day
for your yearly date.
It could be the first day of spring, Flag Day,
or the anniversary of your first date.
Plan the events of the day and include
some special traditions that fit the day.

Don't let anyone or anything intrude on this day.
Protect it and cherish it.
It will be the date that gives you the most
treasured memories you will ever have.

LifeMates
A Lover's Guide
for a Lifetime Relationship

By Dr. Dave and Jan Congo

Dave and Jan Congo provide an exciting lover's guide for a lifetime relationship by exploring 13 key characteristics of a healthy marriage. LifeMates brings proven hope to real marriage issues and helps couples make daily, deliberate choices to build up and nurture each other and their marriage. ISBN: 0-78143-693-1

They Call Me
Mr. Romance
A Business Man's Guide
to Romancing Your Wife

By Michael Keyes

Sometimes hard-edged, sometimes hysterical, Mike Keyes tells it like it is (and was) in his own straight-talking, no-nonsense style. This is no ordinary marriage book – Keyes lays out his life, mistakes and all, revealing a successful business man who could close multi-million dollar deals at the office, but still somehow miss the mark at home. . . that is, until he became "Mr. Romance." ISBN: 0-78143-691-5